THE PLAN E

Overcoming life's challenges with a **smile**

"Accept life as it is. As it is, whatever life is there, accept. Don't retaliate, don't get angry, don't get upset. Just accept. And you will enjoy the same life which was irritating you! You will see the enjoying part of that. And it will be so beautiful the way you will see that you will get over all your problems. You will get over all your enemies. And a kind of a very fresh, beautiful existence you will have."

HHSM

THE E PLAN

Nigel Powell

ISBN 978-0-9548519-3-4

"I ate, I drank, I was merry. Now what?"

PART ONE

WELCOME

"Fine. Just grin then."

Dear Sir or Madam,

Thank you very much for signing up to our new, all inclusive Evolution Plan (E Plan). We hope you will find it useful, and that by deploying it in all aspects of your life you will gain the kind of spiritual and personal growth that you seek.

As a short introduction, we are writing to you to confirm the details of available options, which includes the free bolt-on extra of an all-inclusive lifetime guarantee. (see below)

POINT 1

As a Premium Member of the E Plan, we confirm that you have access to any of the following methods of spiritual growth through tapasya and trial.

OPTIONS

A. Work Issues

B. Financial Issues

C. Relationship Issues

D. Health Issues

E. **Left Sided Issues** (e.g. lethargy, depression etc)

F. **Right Sided Issues** (e.g. stress, hypertension etc)

G. **General Illusion Issues** (aka Maya Syndrome)

As you know, you are allowed to select any option you require, to provide the personal tests you need to introspect and grow, with the proviso that you must select a minimum of one and a maximum of two options only.

POINT 2

By agreeing to enrol on this program, you understand that you will be subject to an increasingly intense level of testing as your personal evolution progresses. The more detached, compassionate and spiritually oriented you become, the more you will find your specific option/s will test you.

This is normal behaviour and is built into the system to ensure you obtain the maximum benefit from your membership. Please do not be alarmed if some of your tests push your emotions and fortitude to their limits. It's all part of the exquisitely structured process. Try to think of it as a custom personal car wash and valet. Without the suds.

POINT 3

Please note that the tests you will receive during the duration of your membership will not necessarily be limited to the option/s you select. While these will be the main focus of your testing, other tests will be included in the program to ensure you gain a wide ranging education on all matters relating to your spiritual ascent.

POINT 4

As per our standard terms and conditions, members may at any time withdraw from their membership with immediate effect simply by ticking the: *'Retire From All'* box on the relevant Policy Document form.*

"You fetch and you fetch and you fetch, and then one day then you start to wonder if it will ever be enough."

At this point all tests, trials and tapasya will cease and the member will revert to a conventional life without spiritual significance or reward. Further details on this option can be obtained on request by emailing info@dontbeasillybilly.edu.

POINT 5

Each member on the program will receive a specially customised series of tests to pass over time. Each test will be rigorously evaluated beforehand in order to deliver the specific insight or understanding needed for the member to progress to the next level. For this reason, members are not encouraged to apply generic solutions or answers to the test they face, as it may result in less than optimum results, as well as an uneasy sense of deja vu later on.

Stop thinking and end your problems. Lao Tse

POINT 6

Each of the tests in the chosen option/s will be re-applied to the member in different situations until this test is passed. The test will, however, be adjusted each time to present a new challenge. The tests may be re-run a number of times in quick succession where there is persistent misunderstanding. These repeats will occur until the member realises their mistake, and takes inner steps to overcome their problem and move on. Members may want to enjoy this process as if it were a series of mock exams. Without the messy Post-It note reminders.

POINT 7

Members are reminded that selection of Option d. (Health Issues) may, depending on subtle desire and other factors, result in an unexpected and unwanted transition into an incorporeal state ahead of time. Members are warned to bear this in mind before making this a part of their overall program choice. Members in any doubt should spend some time reviewing their full understanding of the nature of Samsara before proceeding to make any final decisions.

POINT 8

While we can make no promises about the rate of progress of each individual member, please rest assured that our regular Lifetime Guarantee still applies. As long as any member continues to conduct their meditation practice and other observances as suggested by the literature, they will continue to reap the spiritual, mental and physical benefits that the E Plan delivers.

Each member is responsible for ensuring they maintain full attention on their practice, and do not become distracted from their chosen path. Excuses such as, 'I had my driving test', or 'there was a good movie on', should probably be reserved for other more mundane situations.

All tests depend on diligent regular meditation occuring at all times during the duration of the individual's membership. It is important to remember that without this, things may get rather messy, rather quickly.

POINT 9

If at any point any member believes they have not received the expected level of spiritual growth, they should first check to ensure that their practice is currently fulfilling the criteria set out above, and also that their desire remains as strong as when they first signed up to the E Plan.

Should all things seem to be in order, and the member still believes they are not receiving their due reward, they may opt to do one of two things.

a) They may wish to re-evaluate their expectations to determine whether it is realistic to expect such a rapid return on their investment. Instant nirvana is not generally a result of a desire to evolve. Even for very nice people!

b) If the member still feels aggrieved, they can return to their Policy Document Form and tick the 'Retire From All' box. At this point their membership will immediately be cancelled. We regret that due to the subtle nature of the membership terms, we are unable to offer any refunds of time, effort, desire or outcome upon termination of membership.

POINT 10

Members are respectfully reminded that having 'Retired' from the program, they may find it increasingly difficult to re-engage and return to the program in the future. While there have been cases of past members successfully restoring their membership, it does take a significant degree of humility, patience and self-awareness to successfully resume a program of trial and tapasya once again. This is especially true of those with rugged good looks, a hefty trust fund or a large Instagram following.

POINT 11

Members are actively encouraged to interact, support, teach and learn from other members on the program. Each member brings a particular quality to the program, and so can deliver a unique and valuable contribution when asked. Cooperation between members is in fact a fundamental key to succeeding in the program over the long term. Some of the most important insights and understanding will come from day to day interaction with other individuals on the same journey.

POINT 12

In very rare cases members may be permitted to switch their first choice of Plan to a different Plan (or

Plans). In this case, the original test structure will be altered and a new set of challenges will immediately be applied. Members are gently reminded that a switch of options will not result in any lesser intensity of test, only in a different set of issues, which may serve to present even more of an obstacle to a successful resolution. Where at all possible, members are advised to stick with their original choice of Plan/s in order to maintain continuity and consistency of the education over time.

POINT 13

All events are tests of some type, however it is only the most challenging ones which offer the enlightened progress that is the keynote of the program. However it should be noted that success in ancillary challenges can count towards each member's overall score when it comes to making a transition from one level to a higher one. And, sadly, vice versa.

POINT 14

Cheating the system is impossible.

© MARK ANDERSON, WWW.ANDERTOONS.COM

"So it's not enough that I pollinate the roses?
Now I'm supposed to stop and smell them too?!"

POINT 15

Membership of the program continues until such time as the member either:

A. Transitions into an expected or unexpected incorporeal state

B. Elects to tick the 'Retire From All' box on the Policy Document form

C. Transitions into a significantly elevated state of spiritual awareness, otherwise known as Nirvana (or Moksha if you're not a fan of loud rock music).

Once any of these states is reached, membership for this period automatically terminates, and the individual will inhabit their new position until further notice. Please note that c. is an extremely rare occurrence at this time, and should not be chosen as a particular goal of the program so as to avoid any possibility of disappointment.

POINT 16

In line with Clause 15, we encourage Members to look upon the membership itself as the most satisfying aspect of the journey, rather than focus on any of the optional (or inadvertent) termination conditions. This will avoid unnecessary emotional turmoil which may in itself result in sub-optimal performance of any challenge or task. In other words, it is strongly recommended that Members keep their eye OFF the prize.

POINT 17

The Plan does not recognise failure as a ... well failure. Members do not fail, they instead encounter a new opportunity to learn. Members are reminded that without obstacles, there is no learning, and without learning there is no evolution. And we all know what happens if there is no evolution. We become accountants. (no offense). Members are therefore strongly encouraged to remember that 'failing' a test is not a condemnation of the individual any more than being unable to open a jar of pickles is a sign of weakness. We may just have to learn to use a dish cloth better.

Life is a series of natural and spontaneous changes. Don't resist them - that only creates sorrow. Lao Tse

PART TWO PLAN OPTIONS

"I dunno, doc... Am I a good girl? I mean deep down?"

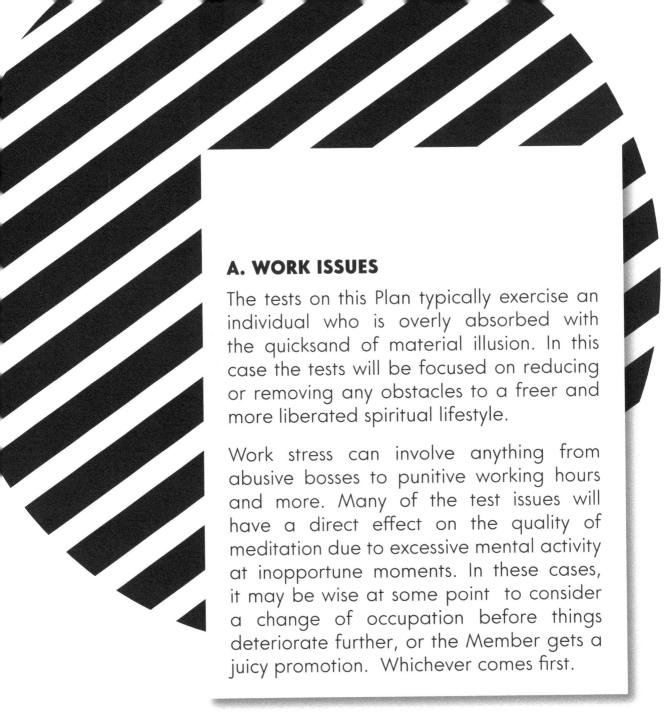

A. WORK ISSUES

The tests on this Plan typically exercise an individual who is overly absorbed with the quicksand of material illusion. In this case the tests will be focused on reducing or removing any obstacles to a freer and more liberated spiritual lifestyle.

Work stress can involve anything from abusive bosses to punitive working hours and more. Many of the test issues will have a direct effect on the quality of meditation due to excessive mental activity at inopportune moments. In these cases, it may be wise at some point to consider a change of occupation before things deteriorate further, or the Member gets a juicy promotion. Whichever comes first.

Passing the tests at this stage often also require courage; both to change circumstances (and maybe financial security too – see below) and/or approaches to workloads and demands. Those who report having passed these tests, suggest that a strong heart, and confident and bold actions, will often make the difference between success and failure.

At the end of the day, a job, no matter how elevated, secure and remunerative, is only a means to an end. Which makes it perhaps easier to deal with as a test, in contrast to other more subtle E Plan options. However, it should be remembered that where our members are engaged in prestigious or valuable professions, the challenges can be just as intense as in any other option. Again, in these cases, a renewed

> *Top Tip: Entering into politics as a work choice may be inadvisable in many circumstances, especially for those with large Instagram followings.*

focus on meditation and surrender will be the only safe method of passing the tests being delivered.

B. FINANCIAL ISSUES

Premium Members who are undergoing financial stress testing may find it hard to separate out reality from fiction in these cases. Money is such a fundamental part of the conventional lifestyle, that any serious financial trouble is likely to trigger an immediate and unbalanced shift to the right side. Unfortunately if left unaddressed this can then lead to a damaging slump into the left side as things get worse. Not a roller-coaster so much as a wobbly seesaw of bewilderment.

One very effective way of passing this type of test is to lose or reduce the attachment for material goods, and to consciously retreat back to a life of deliberate simplicity. This will have an added bonus of forcing a more humble and compassionate approach to life in general. Note: hankering after a small cave with a snowy porch may be taking things a step too far.

Severe financial hardship, involving loss of home, livelihood, family cohesion and suchlike may be the result of a continuous failure to detach from job or possessions in some way or another. A tussle between the Ego and Spirit perhaps? Where there is already detachment in place, there may be other reasons why the test is creating the hardship being suffered. A tiny and deeply buried dash of self-deception also cannot be ruled out. In each case the goal of the Member is to identify the root cause of the test, pass it and move on.

There is no quick fix to financial challenges, just a growing power of witnessing and a focus on joy and love rather than earnings and position. It can be hard to undertake at first, but after a time it becomes easier to understand that this simpler, more engaged approach to life can deliver a very benevolent outcome. Members who are already millionaires, may wish to consider selling a yacht and spending more time in the company of needy children. This may be somewhat therapeutic.

To the mind that is still, the whole universe surrenders. Lao Tse ───────

© MARK ANDERSON, WWW.ANDERTOONS.COM

ANDERSON

"I'd like less of an emotional roller coaster and more of a teacup ride."

C. RELATIONSHIP ISSUES

This option is highly recommended both for its effectiveness and its ability to deliver other benefits at the same time. The relationship tests thrown up by this option, include everything from parental pressure to mental and physical aggression from spouses and/or family and so on. In each case, the test will require significant degrees of detachment and compassion, otherwise the test will have to be repeated until a successful pass is achieved.

One of the main difficulties of overcoming this series of tests, is the degree to which relationships are embedded in every crevice of our existence. No parent, spouse, sibling, boss, employee, friend, stranger or Great Aunt is spared.

To maximise the chance of passing the tests in this option, the individual should first determine whether any factors in their own personality may be triggering the relationship issues in question. Once they have done that, they can then start to introspect on how to overcome the issue in question, aiming for the most loving outcome.

It is likely that the early tests in this option will involve relatively trivial matters, and progress over time (and successful completion) to significantly more difficult challenges; including infidelity, intense outbursts of anger, drug use, and even open attacks on the nature of a spiritual practice. Most of the feedback received from members who have passed this test suggest that strong levels of detachment, generated by deeply sincere meditation can be a winning approach. This strategy, which also involves a long cool look inside the heart for answers, appears to yield extremely good results in cases where the relationship is based around an emotional connection. Love is the core of the solution, which requires patience, respect and a good dash of humble pie.

Divorce – or getting fired from your job - may be an indication that a relationship test is not going quite as well as could be expected. Which also may trigger consequences of a spiritual kind (including involuntary switching to other Plans / tests). However there is no need to panic!

One of the most severe tests in a relationship can be a death in the family, which at the most extreme can shake one's spiritual beliefs to the core. There is no simple quick fix to this type of test. They involve such intense emotional impacts that we are often punched back to the root of our very existence. As with any of these premium level trials - which include severe problems with our children – members are typically advised to fall back on the one thing which can carry them through the fire. Faith. This is the faith that we are not wrong or being punished, that the pain will pass, and a faith that we can cut through the illusion and find truth instead of pain. As the Lord Buddha said, "Pain is certain, suffering is optional."

One of the strongest means of overcoming this form of tapas is to seek the help and counsel of others in the community. In these cases group attention can be put on the problem to seek a solution. In fact some of the most effective relationship solutions will generally involve multiple parties working together to dig out love and compassion from the smoking embers of an angry, fractured or grief stricken heart.

Extreme life trauma is never an easy thing to endure or to transcend, but it does indicate that the member is a strong enough personality to rise above the challenge. It takes faith, dedication and a deep understanding of the pattern and cycle of life to help it all make sense. In these cases, meditation – diligent, thoughtless, deep meditation – is the number one tool members can use to fight back against the anxiety, depression, stress or traumatic grief they may be facing. Remember too that time heals!

"Meow. There, I said it and I'm glad."

D. HEALTH ISSUES

Selecting heath as your spiritual growth engine is one of the most direct, but at the same time difficult, methods of achieving personal evolution. The ability to detach oneself from physical infirmity, sometimes over the long term, is extremely difficult in every way. This is especially true since the pain that often accompanies such affliction can be more than enough to obstruct meditation and impair our attention. For this reason this option is only suggested as a last resort, when other options have been exhausted.

There are two simple rules to use when attempting to pass typical Health tests:

1. Have patience. In general we can say that routine health issues come and go as part of the pattern of life. Especially in the early days of our evolution, the level of ailment that is likely to be triggered for the ascent may be mild. It may also run its own course over a reasonable time period, and without any intervention. In this case just stay calm and watch things work out.

2. Don't blame yourself. There are many different reasons why we could be hit with ill health,

and of course we should try to identify the root cause and treat it – as well as the symptoms - as effectively as possible.   But the problem could start with any part of the subtle system. It might even be a matter of karma, lifestyle, environment or family, or it could be something as simple as over stressing about our lack of Instagram followers.

The general rule is don't just treat the symptoms, treat the cause. We may need to footsoak in the evening, change our diet, stop doing something which is battering our psyche. Whatever it is, we generally should be able to identify it fairly quickly and start to take steps.

The story is different with more chronic ailments of course. Members are advised to tackle these trials with utmost seriousness, using whatever conventional and alternative medical options that are available. At the same time the need to pay extra attention to subtle causes and remedies should not be forgotten.

Should the individual continue to grow in spiritual stature, then the tests are likely to intensify, at which point the use of more powerful meditation techniques is recommended. This will require full attention and faith regarding the use of these vibrational resources. It cannot be stressed enough how important strong and open hearted faith in the healing power of the subtle system is in these cases. The test may be passed by using conventional medical technologies, but the discrimination and strength to proceed along the right course will come from the Member's own spiritual stability.

Do remember that while conventional medicines may well cure the ailment very quickly, it may also leave the underlying test unfulfilled, which suggests it may return in another format later on. Again this does not imply we are being punished, just that we need to pass the test and move on to a more subtle level.

E. LEFT SIDED ISSUES (E.G. LETHARGY, DEPRESSION ETC)

Premium members have the option of selecting an option which focuses on specific aspects of their general personality. Left sided issues, for example, will include things such as lethargy or depression, which can result in many different trials and effects. Members may find it more difficult to meditate regularly, or they may simply have a problem buttering toast. Many of the tests which will be delivered in this option involve inaction or inattention to the basic necessities of life. This is especially true when the test involves losing interest in the spiritual journey completely. In these cases the strongest method of passing the test in question is to revert to the techniques which offer most relief to an over cooled left side.

"I dunno, maybe deep down I *want* to bark up the wrong tree."

The use of sunlight, heat and the proper diet are all tools which can help to repel left sided tests and challenges. By maintaining a positive attitude, the individual can overcome the inertia and lack of self-belief which can cause a regression in spiritual progress. In severe cases, a period spent engaging more regularly and fully with the spiritual community is recommended as a solution. This may be easier said than done, but it is definitely an extremely valuable option if used.

F. RIGHT SIDED ISSUES (E.G. STRESS, HYPERTENSION ETC).

This option often ties in with the Work tests, in that stress is usually easily generated through employment or financial issues. The kind of problems which are associated with this option include anger issues, dissatisfaction with all aspects of living and a general hostility or dominating attitude to others in the family or community in general.

There are a number of well tried methods of passing these tests, many of which involve increased exposure to a more tranquil environment, and increased focus on meditation and quiet introspection.   In many cases, even a simple change of occupation can help overcome the tests quickly and effectively. Where this is not possible, moving location can help, even temporarily. A weekend vacation in nature can be a real rejuventator in the right circumstances. Especially when combined with the right kind of pure desire. Of course doing regular meditation every day is an extremely powerful way of restoring and maintaining balance.

Do note, repeated inability to overcome this test can quickly lead to a shift to a new option - such as adverse Health issues or worse. In these cases drinking alcohol - especially very large glasses of tepid brown ale - is not recommended, as this may cause unexpectedly wobbly side effects.

Once again, the challenge for members is to identify the cause of the stress/over excitement and deal with it as effectively as possible. The test itself will provide clues as to the root solution, and through meditation this can be uncovered and recognised. At that point, half the battle is won. It is hard to stay angry if we realise that our eating and sleeping habits may be contributing to the problem, and we need to slow down a bit to compensate and cure.

G. GENERAL ILLUSION ISSUES (AKA MAHA MAYA SYNDROME).

Sometimes there is no clear cut compartment into which we can place a test. It will not fit solely into any of the foregoing categories or it combines parts of each. Or it is simply unexplainable. In these cases we can think of the test as part of a general confrontation with the illusory state of being, the mystical and mythical Maya. That's not to say the test is any less real to the member who is experiencing the trial. On the contrary, the tests which are difficult to understand can be the most intense ones. Why has something happened to me? What did I do wrong? This doesn't make sense. This is impossible. All of these observations and more can indicate that the member is undergoing a trial from this particular option.

Once again, the basic rules remain the same. Keep calm and carry on. These tests may not be as specific as those involving family, money or health, but they can be just as intense. Members are advised to avoid selecting this plan unless they are particularly resilient to change, because these tests typically involve a lot of uncertainty. Because the cause can be hard to identify, the early signals can very very confusing, and the member may experience long periods of agonising indecision, as they try to figure out what the heck is going on. This is not a great recipe for a peaceful night's sleep.

The good news is that with patience, things will gradually become clearer. Every meditation will bring more insights, possible solutions and outcomes. The member will slowly learn what it is they are being tested on, and which issues this particular trial addresses. The root causes may be more esoteric or mundane, but the test will require the same level of faith and diligence as all of the other plans. This option can be thought of as a 'Miscellaneous' issues plan, which sweeps up many of life's most bizarre episodes and delivers them as direct tests of our spiritual strength. How we react will determine how easily we progress to the next level in our evolution. So nothing new here.

Be content with what you have;
rejoice in the way things are.
When you realize there is nothing
lacking, the whole world belongs
to you. Lao Tse

PART THREE
PLAN
OF
ACTION

"I SAID I THINK YOU MIGHT HAVE SOME AVOIDANCE ISSUES!!"

IMMEDIATELY

a member senses that they are the subject of a major test, a number of important things apply. First, they should remember that they have not necessarily done anything 'wrong' in a conventional sense. Their trial could be triggered by any number of factors, including past karmas, so the best approach is to stay calm and introspect on the situation at hand. In this way the member can identify which option test he or she is facing, and then adopt the necessary mental, emotional and situational attitude to pass the exam.

The key point is to recognise that there is almost certainly a deep seated issue which is the vehicle for the test. Members can think of it as a vulnerability, something which we need to lose in order to move onwards and upwards in our spiritual growth. Sometimes this issue is not obvious, or we have become expert in burying it, in which case members are advised to relax and surrender to the power of meditation in order to flush it to the surface so it can be recognised and dealt with.

In most cases 'dealing' with the issue at the core of the test is simply a matter of surrendering ourselves to the outcome, without seeking any particular result. This works because it is a supreme test in itself – a sort of meta test. To surrender requires a huge leap of faith, as well as a heightened detachment to the circumstances of our current trial. The combination of these factors are incredibly powerful in elevating us to a new level, and in many cases we can actually feel ourselves grow, both subtly and as a personality, while the test is progressing.

Another key to success is for the member to cultivate a deeply embedded sense of patience. All trials become less traumatic with the passage of time, and in fact for many of them time is actually the key to passing the test. Our human nature is to expect or demand instant solutions to our ills. The Pavlovian ding of the microwave oven has driven us to expect a whole host of 5 minute fixes. The success of the pharmaceutical and medical industries is largely built around this expectation, so it is not surprising that we become agitated when things don't move as fast as we would like. Instant noodles have a lot to answer for!

But patience is a very powerful antidote to stress

and anguish, simply because it comes with some very important features. We need patience as the foundation to detachment and surrender, which in turn are vital components of passing many trials. We also use patience to give us the time to introspect on our situation. If we aren't patient, then we can easily end up rushing around trying to 'fix' things, instead of working out exactly what we need to fix, and how. The wisest farmers know this to be a truth. "Do nothing, observe everything" as the venerable and wise Masanobu Fukuoka said.

A good question to ask at this point may be 'what's the worst that can happen?' and then explore that journey as a means of gaining some valuable perspective. In most cases the answer will not be life-threatening in any way, at which point the member may realise that they can relax a little more and just let things take their course as they should.

> *Top Tip: members should preferably not over-react - or react at all - to a test in progress. Reaction can often make a situation worse. A calm, centered response, just watching the issue unfold without thinking, often resolves things very effectively. We call this the Teflon State - where issues just slide off you like a friend egg off a buttered pan.*

Note that despite the use of the word 'plan', it is probably not necessary to draw up a schedule, Gantt chart or other tool in order to succeed. In fact plans are often a hindrance, especially when it comes to dealing with the uncertainty of a test. Of course we can plan to improve our situation, but the actual details of that strategy are more than likely going to be hidden from us until our introspection delivers the solution or direction we need to take. Just make sure to look out for the answers as they arrive. Like Great Aunt Lucy on a duck hunt, they may arrive wearing camouflage.

The key to growth is the introduction of higher dimensions of consciousness into our awareness. Lao Tse

HINTS AND TIPS ON PASSING TESTS

"You know, research suggests that purring, even if you're in a bad mood, can help you feel better."

Key Tip

MEDITATION. Without a doubt, the number one single most important tip of all time for anyone facing a major life test is to meditate. Meditate. Meditate. Words cannot stress how important it is to stay in balance and connected during these times of trial. Without it, we are like grass blown in the wind. With it, we become as resilient as the strongest bamboo. We don't meditate because we are desperate, we do it so we can overcome any challenge with detachment and serenity. By staying balanced in this way we make the best decisions, and act as a rock of wisdom for those around us.

Members should not, however, mistake diligence for obsessive fanaticism. In other words, we should try not to meditate obsessively or for unnaturally long periods to force the pace of a solution. Balance is everything. We can and should use advanced techniques whenever possible, but at the same time we must avoid using meditation as a mere prop to get the solution we think we need. Instead we can just wait for the best solution to emerge naturally. It will. In time.

One suggestion we have for members while they're waiting is to take up a hobby. Crochet or croquet are just two that spring to mind. Other pastimes may be better suited for those seeking a less frantic lifestyle.

Generic Tips

EXCUSES. Members are reminded that attempting to pass a test by making excuses cannot be accepted by the E Plan administration. Excuses such as 'no time to meditate', a 'distracting event at work' or other similar proposals will probably only serve to placate the member's Ego, while complicating the chances of future success. The member is strongly advised to really just suck it up and get on with the program. Man.

FANATICISM. It has been noticed in the past that certain members have unfortunately become so lost in the pursuit of their spiritual evolution that they have resorted to extreme asceticism to try and pass their tests and please the administration. Activities such as 10 hour meditations, 5 day candle treatments and reciting huge, obscure texts out loud 3 times a week in the original Sanskrit are examples of such extremes. Wherever possible it should be noted that while tapasya is good for the soul, extreme efforts are almost always counter-productive, as they engage the Ego and reduce the joy. Which can be fatal to passing any further tests.

LETHARGY. There have been reports of members experiencing profound periods of laziness. This is highly discouraged as a means to achieve spiritual evolution. The typical recommended solution, should this occur, is a combination of bright natural or artificial light, a renewed love and respect for multiple candles, and very loud rock music. Or Beethoven if wigs are more to taste.

BENEVOLENCE. It may be useful to remember that all tests are delivered as a form of benevolence, for the spiritual elevation of the individual. Raging against 'failure' or the difficult nature of the test will probably not prove to be productive. And in fact it may be very distracting. Members are advised instead to seek the joy in all tests where possible. A mantra a day can help keep the ego at bay.

DIFFICULTY AND CHOICE. Your custom crafted artisanal tests are specifically designed to challenge resolve and improve your ability to rely on faith at times of duress. For that reason members are encouraged to practice seeking out difficult options at all times, especially when faced with a choice of an easy or hard route. This will give them practice in the art of weathering a storm. Please note, this does not mean that fanatic asceticism is a valid option. Long stretches of time spent on a bleak frozen mountain in Siberia may not deliver the kind of happiness or liberation you are expecting at all.

New beginnings are disguised as painful endings. Lao Tse ────────

"So you believe that when you flap your wings on one side of the planet, all kinds of crazy things are caused on the other side? That sounds like a lot of responsibility."

INTROSPECTION. One of the common questions received from members is what tactic is most effective in overcoming tests. While every individual is different, one technique which has continually proven to be very effective is that of introspection. By employing the art of deep and genuine self-enquiry, members should eventually identify the reason, history and options for each test they face. Avoid apportioning blame to anyone or any agency, and simply treat the trial as the opportunity to grow and learn that it is. Alternatively, it might be helpful to do a Google search. (Just kidding!)

EGO. At the end of the day, almost all tests – especially at the beginning of our journey – will involve the ego in one form or another. Whether it is our mistaken belief that we are in control, a delusion of competence or any one of a myriad of mental contortions, our ego is a master of trickery. And so any path to spiritual growth will necessarily involve tests to help us navigate around the constraints of our mind and ego. What makes this particularly important is the fact that our ego excels at playing tricks. We can believe we are not acting on behalf of our egotism, even when it is absolutely clear that we are. Only our meditation can take us out of this delusion, and even then we have to be strong enough, and perceptive enough, to recognise the truth – even when we don't like it.

FAITH. Nothing is as important to our spiritual growth as the right amount and type of faith. It may sound like a cliché, but it is our faith that carries us through the worst tests and gives us something to hang on to when it feels like we're drowning. The quality of this faith is absolutely crucial. It has to be without motive, and without desire for a particular outcome. In its purest form it has to embody surrender to the joy of any result. This is true liberation. This type of faith understands that this Maha Maya has ultimate benevolence baked in, even if we don't see it or can't recognise it. It's a faith that keeps our attention locked onto a Divine purpose even when things are at their darkest, and not though some form of masochism or guilt, but because we have no doubt that we are on a journey of the Spirit. Of evolution.

DETACHMENT. This element is the second component of the crucial trifecta: faith, detachment and surrender. We have to be detached before we can start to see the wood from the trees. We need detachment as a foundation in order to make the best decisions for passing our tests. If we are not detached from a situation, then we are at risk of being consumed by the trauma. Once that happens, we revert to being the servant of our emotions or mental contortions, which can obscure the truth of a situation and fool us into making bad decisions. Detachment doesn't mean being callous and uncaring, it means compassionate witnessing. Pragmatic concern with balance. We are all instinctively detached already; about the small things. We just need to move it up a notch so we are can also be detached about the big bits.

By letting it go it all gets done. The world is won by those who let it go. Lao Tse

SURRENDER. We tend to be pushed into understanding surrender only after many experiments with failure. We are reared to believe we are in charge, that if we don't do something we lose. If we don't study we fail. If we don't work hard we starve. And so on. So the idea of surrender sits uneasily in our belief system. But as a Premium member of the most wonderful E Plan it is essential that we equip ourselves with the maximum amount of surrender that a psyche can carry. It is acquired through practice, meditation and experience. The more we test it out and find it works, the more we feel confident in deploying it again. Of course it's extremely difficult in the beginning to have the faith that things will work out, and many times they don't appear to. But eventually we learn that with this benevolent and intelligent agency surrounding us, we're safe to sit back and relax most times when it counts. Unless there's a fire! At which point we should really surrender to the urge to run away. Quickly.

JOY. The purpose of every journey of spiritual evolution is to experience the joy of existence. This joy in every type of situation is the ultimate liberation, and it is bound up with all of the major states of an unfettered existence; including love, peace and balance. Without enjoyment, our existence is just a dry pursuit of emptiness. Joy fulfils the needs of our Spirit, it gives us purpose and reason. Joy is not happiness, it goes beyond mental experience, it is eternal and ethereal. Our tests are overcome when we can find joy in any outcome, whether we desire it or not. Joy is simple, silent and beautiful.

LOVE. A great many tests are passed quickly and easily with the proper deployment of one of the most powerful – and ironically ridiculed – forces the world has ever known. Marmite. We jest. Love. The power of love – true love, not Hollywood style – dissolves barriers, removes obstacles, builds relationships, engenders trust and respect and heals wounds faster than a 10 ton truck full of antiseptic plasters. Real love has to come from deep within the heart, unconditionally and with no complications. In its purest form it is the driving force of our species; maternal, fraternal and eternal. We don't fall in love, we grow in it. The purest pleasure is to give it, not receive it; although we must be prepared to recognise when we are blessed with its gift. The media may have tried to cheapen it, but all of us know - instinctively and primordially - that it is the building block of existence. Our challenge is to learn how to recognise, deploy and accept it every day of our lives. In this way, tests of any kind will become inconsequential.

I have just three things to teach: simplicity, patience, compassion. These three are your greatest treasures. Lao Tse

© MARK ANDERSON, WWW.ANDERTOONS.COM

"I feel like I'm able to forgive. It's the forgetting that's the issue."

HELP, I CANNOT REMEMBER SIGNING UP FOR THE E PLAN.

That's perfectly normal. Your choice of plan is not made consciously, it happens as a subconscious part of your sign-up process to the spiritual journey. Your spirit is the chariot which accepts the terms and conditions of the program, and it is your desire which is the chauffeur. The options/s you select will in large part be determined by your most important spiritual needs. Your karma may also play a part, as will the ultimate desire for evolution that you contain in your personality. There are also other factors which determine your choices, which are extremely private and so we won't reveal them here. Safe to say they have nothing to do with tagging your face on Instagram.

WHY DO WE NEED TO PASS TESTS?

Simply put, it does us good. By facing and overcoming challenges we gain insight into our strengths and weaknesses, we learn about our true inner priorities and we establish the context of our lives. Challenges make us better beings. Without tests we can become indolent and rootless, without purpose or meaning. That's not to say that everyone is suited to a life of challenges. For some, the mere act of buttering toast is enough excitement for any single lifetime. We all need to choose on which side of the butter knife we stand. Or sit.

WHAT DOES SPIRITUAL EVOLUTION ACTUALLY MEAN?

Evolution implies improvement, a change for the better, and so we can think of spiritual evolution as our journey to grow into a more spiritually aware personality. In its ultimate form this would imply a state beyond illusion, where our personality exists in a form liberated from the shackles of the material world. Or buttering toast. For most of us, however, spiritual evolution means that we try to become better people; more balanced, more loving and compassionate and more appreciative of the subtle aspects of being a human being.

HOW DO I BECOME A MEMBER?

Good news. Membership is open to any human being with a pulse and a desire to take a journey of personal evolution. No qualifications are needed, nor is there any requirement to attend a 'good' school or get a 'good' degree. The prime requirements for membership are a pure heart and a willingness to learn from mistakes. Without guilt or blame. Successful members also focus on the enjoyment of the journey rather than focusing on the end result, as this can complicate decisions and actions during the most testing moments. Success is not measured by fancy diplomas but by inner peace.

HOW DOES THE PROGRAM WORK?

Simple. Members sign on to the program using a quill pen fashioned from the wing feathers of a rare Abyssinian parakeet, and from that moment onwards they agree to accept any number of personally customised tests in their lives. These tests are specially constructed to help the member evolve in the most efficient manner possible. There are no invigilators or examiners, the only judges are the members themselves. They will know what the results of a particular test are, whether it has been passed or not. Inner serenity, and a feeling of ego-less accomplishment, are good indicators that a test has been passed. A headache may indicated the opposite. Please note, a promotion at work does not necessarily reflect a positive outcome.

CAN I CHANGE OPTIONS?

The rules on this are fairly clear. While it is not generally recommended (for reasons of continuity) a member may elect to switch options during the course of a lifetime. In some cases this switch may be involuntary, if it is apparent that the member's personal circumstances have changed to the extent that the current option will no longer be optimally effective. It must be understood that switching options will in no way provide a short cut, or easier route to personal spiritual evolution. Constant changes may in fact make things very tricky indeed.

WHICH OPTION SHOULD I CHOOSE?

Members should select the option they feel will give them the best chance of elevating their spiritual awareness in a balanced way. Of course it's hard to know what this might be without actually experiencing some of the tests first, however that's just the gamble we take in life eh? Unfortunately there is no 'try before you buy' option. Mind you that's true in life itself, so no surprises. One option is for the member to write out all the options onto little pieces of white paper, shuffle them up in a hat and do a random pick. It may not be elegant, but it's a great way to pass time on a rainy Sunday afternoon.

CAN I REQUEST LOW INTENSITY TESTS?

Mmm ... looking for an easy option seldom delivers the kind of shout-out results that we can chat about with the neighbours. However it's fair to say that the tests under each plan do start at a relatively low intensity to help beginners find their feet. The object is not to demotivate members, but to encourage them to continue on, by allowing for constant small wins at each level. That said, there will come a time when the tests will start to push the limits of endurance, rather like a pretty tough triathlon. By that point though, members should definitely know what to expect. Simple answer? Don't be nervous, dive right in.

"What if we focused on changing the spots within?"

HOW DO I CANCEL?

Members may retire from the program at any time by ticking the Retire From All box on the Policy Document form.* See above and below. This choice may lead to some unexpected results, at which point members may wish to consult a nearby friend or lawyer for advice on how to proceed in times of uncertainty and weird pancakes.

Policy Document Form: available from info@dontbesuchachicken.net

WHAT HAPPENS IF I DECIDE NOT TO BECOME A MEMBER?

Absolutely nothing. We simply wish you well and trust that you will enjoy your long and secure career, your plump golden Labrador, two delightful children and the small cottage in the country that you saved for and hope to retire to one day, economy permitting. We also hope that your friends will not be anywhere near as patronising as that last sentence.

ISN'T THIS JUST PROMOTING STOICISM?

Stoicism is indeed a distant relative of the E Plan. However there is one crucial difference. Where stoicism posits that human beings need to make the most of things as they are, the E Plan offers members a way to change things to the way they should be. The absence of true joy in stoicism reveals its dry ascetic core, while the Plan aims to deliver joy through challenge. In the end liberation from the pain of tests gives our members the ultimate joy. This is something which is totes worth working for.

WHAT MEDITATION SHOULD I DO?

There are plenty of types around. Just pick one which is not trendy, doesn't charge money and doesn't claim to make you rich, beautiful or irresistible to Instagram followers. Here's a great example for you and Great Aunt Lucy to try out online - http://www.sahajaonline.com.

"Do *you* think another scoop would make you happier?"

CPSIA information can be obtained
at www.ICGtesting.com
Printed in the USA
LVHW010802191118
597620LV00026B/936/P

9 780954 851934